This Book Belongs to:

Printed in the United States of America

Editor: Sharp Editorial, LLC

Paperback ISBN:978-1-956911-10-7
HardCover ISBN:978-1-956911-09-1

Dedication

In life, we encounter good and bad people. When you are young, it's fun to keep secrets with friends, unless it's a secret that may hurt someone's feelings or cause bodily harm.

This book is dedicated to all the young girls and boys, young ladies and men, who have been hurt and told to keep it a secret, those who have been touched inappropriately without permission and afraid to say something.

It is time!

Find someone you trust and spill the beans.
It is never okay to be touched inappropriately.
If they told you they would hurt you
or your family if you told, tell anyway.
If they told you that no one would
believe you, tell anyway.

You are a survivor!

You are not alone.

Shh... Don't Tell

"Good morning, love bug! Your stepbrother will be here today when you get home from school," Riley's mom, Mrs. Cole, said. "He will meet you at your bus stop."

"Yay! Josh is coming over," cheered Riley.

"I'll be glad when your dad returns from his business trip and your sister comes home for Spring Break," Mrs. Cole said. "Then, we will have a full house again! I shouldn't be too late coming home from work. I have leftovers in the fridge for dinner for you and Josh. For now, get ready for school. Make sure your headband matches your clothes, and brush your teeth, please," instructed Mrs. Cole. "And hurry! Your bus will be here soon."

"Yes, Mom," Riley answered, heading toward her room to finish getting ready for school.

***

Later that afternoon, Josh waited for Riley at her bus stop, just as Mrs. Cole had said. As soon as Riley's bus pulled up and she saw Josh, her eyes lit up with excitement. When her bus stopped, Riley ran straight to Josh, giving her brother a big hug.

"I missed you so much, Josh!" Riley exclaimed.

"I missed you too, Riley," Josh smiled.

"I'm starved," Riley said.

"Your mom said there's food in the fridge. I'll put it in the oven for us," Josh said.

As Riley and Josh continued to walk together, Josh looked over at his sister and smiled. "Wow, Riley. You have grown so much. You're becoming a beautiful young lady," he said with excitement. "I was looking for a little girl with plats to get off the bus."

Riley giggled. "Thanks, Josh!"

HOOL BUS

The two began to chat about Riley's day and a few other random topics like the latest music. Finally, they arrived home, and Josh began to prepare the leftover food from the refrigerator.

While sitting at the dinner table, Josh and Riley started to talk again. "So, how's school?" Josh asked. "Fifth grade, right?"

"Boring," Riley sighed. "I can't wait for middle school. Mom says I can wear lip gloss and maybe pick out my clothes," Riley boasted.

"Wait. You don't pick out your clothes?" Josh questioned.

"I know, right?!" Riley replied, feeling frustrated. "It's so unfair. All my friends pick out their clothes," she cried. "Mom and Dad treat me like such a baby."

"Well, I won't treat you like a baby," Josh said.

Suddenly, the kitchen timer buzzed, which meant the lasagna was ready in the oven. Josh and Riley couldn't wait to eat.

Josh carefully removed the tray from the oven and served Riley a piece, then helping himself to a hearty plate.

“This lasagna is the bomb,” Josh said with excitement.

“Lasagna is my favorite,” Riley replied. “Mom always makes it extra cheesy for me.”

The kitchen was silent as Riley and Josh shoveled down the last remaining bites of lasagna.

“I’ll go ahead and clean the kitchen,” Riley offered.

“I’ll help, too!” Josh chimed in. “After all, I helped make the mess.” They both chuckled, looking at the mess of plates and utensils.

In no time at all, the kitchen was clean. The dishes were put away, and there wasn’t a crumb in sight.

“Now to the boring part of my life,” Riley complained. “It’s time for homework.”

"Let me know if you need anything," Josh offered. "It's still early, and besides, I haven't hung out with you in a long time. Can't your homework wait?" Josh asked.

Riley silently debated with herself, realizing she only had a little bit of homework to complete. "Okay," Riley agreed, "but my homework has to be done before Mom gets home, or she will have my butt!"

"Don't worry! I'll make sure you finish it before she gets back," Josh said.

"So, what do you want to do?" Riley asked. "We can play my PlayStation or a board game," she suggested.

"No, those are kiddy games," Josh said.

"No, they're not," Riley argued. "Besides, I'm still a kid. What do you want to do, Mr. Grown Up?" yelled Riley in an aggravated tone.

“Well, I was thinking of something a little bit more fun... but forget it. We can play the kiddy games,” Josh said, sparking Riley’s curiosity.

“Spit it out, Josh,” Riley pleaded. “What’s do you have in mind that’s more fun?”

“The game is called Riding the Bull,” Josh finally revealed, “and this is better than playing PlayStation.”

“Better than PlayStation?” Riley asked in excitement.

“Ten times better,” Josh said, nodding his head. “All the teenagers are playing it.”

“It sounds stupid, but I’ll play,” Riley said, a bit suspicious. “So, how do you play?”

“I have to tell you the rules first,” Josh said. “You must listen very carefully because it’s a secret game for teenagers. You said you want to be treated more like an adult, right?” Josh asked.

"Yeah, duh!" Riley exclaimed. "I hate being treated like a kid."

"You will be the first 11-year-old..." Josh said before Riley interrupted.

"Stop! I'm almost 12. I'm practically a woman," Riley demanded.

"Okay, okay, almost 12-year-old to play this game," Josh finished.

"First, you must promise not to tell anyone, or the chain will be broken. If you tell anyone you played this secret game, one of your family members will die. Once the chain is broken, everyone will know who broke the chain," Josh instructed in a serious tone.

"No way," Riley said in fear. "I'm telling on you!"

"You know what? Let's stick to the kiddy stuff and play the PlayStation," Josh said, feeling frustrated.

"No, no. I want to play! I promise to listen to the rules," cried Riley.

"Fine. Raise your right hand and repeat after me," Josh said. "I, Riley Cole."

"I, Riley Cole," Riley repeated.

"Promise to keep the Riding the Bull game a secret, taking this to my grave. If I tell, I could lose a family member from breaking the chain," Josh said.

Riley repeated the pact, feeling like a grownup.

"That's it!" Josh exclaimed. "Now, let's seal the deal with a pinky promise," he said.

Josh and Riley pinky promised, and she could hardly contain herself.

"Now what?" Riley demanded in excitement.

"First, you have to hide somewhere in the house. If I find you, you have to ride the bull," Josh explained. "Have you ever seen the fake bulls that throw people from side to side? Well, my lap is the bull," Josh said, "so go run and hide."

"I'll make sure I hide well, so you don't find me," Riley said, feeling confident.

As Riley hid, she couldn't help but giggle. Josh just followed the giggles to find his sister.

"I found you," yelled Josh.

"Aw, man!" Riley laughed.

"Well, I found you, so let's go ride the bull," Josh said.

Josh set up a chair in the living room and instructed Riley to straddle her legs over his legs and wrap her feet around the chair so she would not fall.

Once Riley positioned herself, Josh yelled, "Let the ride begin!"

Josh began bouncing and swinging Riley every which way, up and down, all around. Riley was giggling, having a blast. Josh made sure to hold her waist gently, so she did not fall. Finally, after a minute or two, the ride was over.

"One more time, one more time," Riley chanted.

"I took it easy on you that time," Josh laughed.

"I'm not a baby! I promised I can handle it," Riley cried.

"Well, that chair hurt my back," Josh said.

"We can sit on my bed, and then you can bounce me higher," Riley suggested.

"Okay," agreed Josh. "Hide well, Riley. If I find you, you have to ride the bull."

Riley walked through the house on her tippy toes, hoping to find the perfect spot. Although she wanted to ride the bull again, she also wanted to find a great hiding spot.

"He won't find me here," Riley whispered to herself.

A few seconds later, Josh slowly snuck up behind his sister and yelled, "Gotcha!"

Riley's shadow almost jumped out of her skin. All Riley could do was scream out of fear, and she began hitting Josh for scaring her so fiercely.

"It was a good hiding spot," Josh said, trying to reassure his sister. "I found you, though, so... what time is it?" he yelled.

"It's time to ride the bull!" they shouted in unison.

"This time, we will do it a little differently," Josh said. "This time, because you have on your uniform skirt, just take off your panties," he instructed.

"Why?" Riley asked. "I didn't do that last time."

"And I took it easy on you," Josh rudely replied. "Your underwear scratched my leg, so I think it would be easier if you took them off. Plus, you said you wanted to play again, and we can't break the chain. I'm not looking, I promise," Josh swore.

"Okay, fine. They're off," Riley said, following her brother's instructions, placing her underwear on the floor.

"Since we're on the bed, I will wrap my legs around yours," Josh explained. "Now come straddle me."

Seconds later, Riley began feeling very uncomfortable. "Wait, Josh! What's that?" Riley shouted in confusion.

"Calm down. The ride is about to start," Josh said as he began piercing Riley's innocence.

Riley had no idea what was going on, but she felt a pain she had never felt before. "You're hurting me, Josh! Stop! I don't want to ride anymore. Please, stop! I don't like this. Stop!"

Josh began bouncing Riley up and down as she screamed in pain. His legs wrapped around hers and his arms wrapped around her body, bouncing her around until he relieved himself inside her, finally deciding to let her go. Josh had taken Riley's freedom and purity in the blink of an eye.

Riley fell to the floor and balled up in pain with tears rolling down her face, thinking she promised not to tell anyone. She screamed no, but her no fell on deaf ears.

"Was this my fault?" she wondered. "If only I did my homework instead."

Josh stood up, zipped his pants, and laughed. "Why are you crying? You wanted to be treated like a big girl, and now you're a big girl. Oh, and don't forget our pinky promise."

Riley cried even harder when she saw she was bleeding. She stood up and slammed the door as Josh walked out. She knew she needed to be cleaned up before her mom came home, but it hurt to stand. Her ladyhood was taken, and Riley felt awful.

Riley slowly rose from her bedroom floor and went to the bathroom to take a shower. As soon as the water warmed up, Riley stepped into the shower. She tried to scrub all her skin away as she cried and felt guilty about what had happened. The worst part is that she promised not to say a word, or else she would break the chain. Riley could not bear to lose anyone in her family, so she decided to keep this awful game a secret.

Around 8 p.m., Riley's mom arrived home from work, and as Mrs. Cole entered the kitchen, Riley gave her mom the biggest hug, as though she had not seen her in ages.

"You two must have had an awesome time," Mrs. Cole said.

"Dinner was awesome," Josh spoke up and said.

"Thank you! I appreciate you sitting with Riley until I came home. Riley, come to say goodnight to your brother. He's about to leave," Mrs. Cole instructed.

"Bye," yelled Riley, emotionless, from the other room. She did not want to go anywhere near her brother.

"Riley Marie, you know that's rude," Mrs. Cole said. "Give your brother a hug."

Riley walked to the front door, where Josh was standing, now doing as her mother had said. As Riley hugged her brother, Josh whispered in her ear, "Shh, don't tell."

Riley quickly released her arms and rushed off to her room.

"Thanks again," said Mrs. Cole.

"Anytime," Josh replied.

As Mrs. Cole locked the living room door behind Josh, she decided to walk to her daughter's room to remind Riley about bedtime.

"You're in bed at 8:30? Wow, you must be tired," Mrs. Cole said, giving her daughter a warm smile as she saw Riley already tucked in bed.

“Yes, ma’am. Good night,” Riley said, fighting back the tears.

“I guess I will turn in early, too. Your dad will be home tomorrow, thank God,” Mrs. Cole said. “I know he can’t wait to see you! Goodnight, sweetheart,” her mom said as Riley turned over and cried herself to sleep.

***

The next morning, Riley walked downstairs wearing her robe and slippers.

“What’s wrong, Riley?” Mrs. Cole asked. “Why aren’t you getting ready for school?”

“I’m not feeling well, Mom. Can I stay home today?” Riley asked, hoping her mom would agree.

“Is it your sinuses or your stomach?” Mrs. Cole asked, concerned about her daughter’s health.

“Mom, I just want to stay in bed today. Please,” Riley begged.

“Well, let me see if Josh...” Mrs. Cole said before Riley quickly interrupted.

“No!” Riley shouted, stopping her mom mid-sentence. “Josh told me that he had something important to do today. He can’t come over, so we shouldn’t try to call him. Plus, it’s daylight. I can call you if I need you. Dad is on his way home, anyway. I will be fine," Riley said, trying to convince her mom to let her stay home.

"Okay, but if you start feeling worse or need anything, do you promise to call me?" Mrs. Cole asked. "I will be home early anyway. I'm cooking a big dinner to welcome your dad home."

"Sounds good, Mom," Riley said, trying to sound upbeat, even though she was crying on the inside. "I'll see you when you get home from work."

Riley walked upstairs to take another shower. She began to scrub and scrub until her skin was fire red. After she rinsed her body and dried off, Riley crawled back into bed and immediately began to cry. "How could my brother do this to me? I thought he loved me! I hate myself for wanting to be a big girl. Momma always says to pray to make things better. God, if you can hear me, I'm sorry for not listening to my parents and doing my homework after school. Please make this pain go away. Please make Josh go away. Momma said

I'm supposed to love everyone, but how can I love him? Thank you for listening, God. Amen."

Riley cried herself back to sleep, hoping never to wake up.

That afternoon, Riley heard the door open, and she ran down the steps, praying her brother would not walk through the door. Thankfully, it was Mr. Cole, walking inside with his suitcase. His business trip was finally over.

"Daddy!" yelled Riley, relieved her dad was home.

"Hey, Peanut!" Mr. Cole said. "Why aren't you at school?"

"I'm not feeling well," Riley lied, fumbling with her hands. "I'm going back to bed."

"Okay..." Mr. Cole said, finding it strange Riley wasn't in school. After all, Riley loved school. Sure, she didn't love the homework part, but he and Mrs. Cole usually had to order Riley to stay home when she was sick, but today, she was the one who wanted to stay home. It seemed a bit odd to

Mr. Cole. Nevertheless, he set his bags in the living room and walked into the kitchen to grab a cold glass of water.

About an hour later, Mrs. Cole arrived home, excited to see her husband. After their greeting, Mr. Cole asked, “What’s wrong with Riley?”

“I’m not sure,” Mrs. Cole shrugged. “She said she wasn’t feeling well and wanted to stay home, and I agreed to it. Truth be told, I thought she wanted to be here when you arrived. Hopefully, seeing her sister and brother for dinner will cheer her up.”

Later that evening, the doorbell rang. “Hey, Josh!” Mr. Cole said in delight, happy to see his son.

“Hi, Dad! Welcome back. You were gone for like a month,” Josh said, chuckling with his dad.

“Son, it was only two weeks, but it sure felt like a month. I’m thankful for the promotion, but I certainly don’t like traveling for training. When will Monique get here?”

"She should be pulling up shortly," Mrs. Cole chimed in. "I spoke with her a few minutes ago.

"Where is Riley?" Josh asked.

"She wasn't feeling well today," Mrs. Cole answered.

"Do you mind if I check on her?" Josh asked.

"Not at all. Dinner will be ready soon," Mrs. Cole replied.

Josh ran upstairs, knocked on Riley's door, and immediately entered.

"What do you want?" Riley barked. "I didn't say come in!" she cried as tears began to flow down her face.

"Your mom said you weren't feeling well, so I thought I would check on you," Josh said calmly, hoping Riley would lower her tone.

"Get out!" Riley yelled.

“Remember, don’t break the chain,” Josh said as he slowly and quietly walked out the door.

Riley turned over, buried her face into her pillow, and began screaming and crying. “I hate him!” she wailed, wishing she never saw him again.

“Riley said to call her when dinner is ready,” Josh lied as he ran downstairs and saw his dad in the living room.

Five minutes later, Monique walked through the door.

“Hey, everybody!” Monique cheerfully said as she walked inside.

“Monique is here! Let’s eat!” Mr. Cole said.

Monique gave her dad and mom a big hug yet barely acknowledged Josh.

“Hello, Monique,” Josh muttered.

"Why don't you two ever get along?" asked Mrs. Cole.

"Where's Riley?" Monique asked.

"She's upstairs," Mrs. Cole said.

Monique quickly excused herself from the table, quietly snuck up the stairs, and walked into Riley's room, hoping to surprise her.

"Hey, Peanut!" exclaimed Monique, giving her sister a big hug.

"Monique, I'm so happy to see you," cried Riley, relieved her sister was home. "I thought you were coming next week."

"I wanted to surprise you, so you have me for two whole weeks," Monique smiled. "Let's go eat! Dinner is ready."

Monique noticed something was wrong with Riley, but she wanted to wait until they had more one-on-one time. Riley was usually upbeat, smiley, and playful, but today, Riley was quiet and seemed quite sad.

That night, Mrs. Cole served one of her husband's favorite meals – a huge roast with veggies, mashed potatoes, corn, and macaroni and cheese. For dessert, Mrs. Cole baked a homemade apple pie.

Riley was so uncomfortable, she barely ate. Josh kept looking at her and motioning "shh" with his finger. Finally, after everyone was stuffed, the agonizing dinner was over. Josh offered to help clean up, but Mrs. Cole insisted it was the girls' turn to clean the kitchen. Josh gave Mr. and Mrs. Cole a big hug and yelled "goodnight" to his sisters.

"Okay, girls. We're turning in for the night," Mr. Cole said.

Riley walked toward her dad and gave him a big hug.

"I wish you would have eaten more tonight, Peanut," Mr. Cole softly said.

"I know, Daddy. Hopefully, I will feel better tomorrow. Goodnight," Riley said, fighting back her tears.

As the girls began cleaning the kitchen, Monique realized it was the perfect time to ask Riley about her day.

“Riley, what’s wrong?” Monique asked.

“What are you talking about?” Riley asked, trying to seem normal.

“You’re my sister, and I can tell when you’ve been crying,” Monique gently said.

“I wasn’t crying,” Riley lied. “I just wasn’t feeling good today, that’s all,” Riley said, raising her voice.

“Wait, why are you yelling?” Monique asked.

“I’m not,” Riley said, quickly adjusting her tone.

Monique felt the tension in the kitchen and decided to take another approach by asking Riley about school.

“How’s school?” Monique asked.

“Fine,” Riley answered shortly.

“I miss being home, and I miss you,” Monique said, trying to keep the conversation going. “You know, you’re my bestie,” Monique said, trying to get a smile out of her sister.

“No, I’m not,” Riley replied. “You always beat me up.”

“That’s what sisters do,” Monique said, softly nudging her while a smile.

“Well, it looks like we are finished cleaning the kitchen,” Riley said, looking around at the spotless countertops and clean table.

“Let’s go up to your room, and you can start by telling me what’s wrong,” Monique urged. “Is somebody bullying you at school?”

“No!” yelled Riley.

“I know,” Monique smiled. “You like a little boy.”

"No, no, no! Stop asking me. I can't break the chain!" Riley cried.

Monique immediately froze, and tears began to run down her face as Riley ran up to her room and slammed the door. Countless thoughts swirled through Monique's mind. She knew what that phrase meant, and she was devastated her little sister knew, too. Monique took a deep breath and slowly walked to Riley's room.

"Can I come in?" Monique quietly asked as she knocked on Riley's bedroom door.

"Yes," Riley reluctantly agreed.

When Monique walked in, Riley was sitting on the bed, crying.

"Can we talk?" asked Monique. "I'm your big sister, Riley. You can talk to me. I promise nothing will happen to you. Riley, please talk to me," Monique begged.

Riley refused to speak, but Monique knew her sister needed her.

“Okay, I will ask you a question, and you can shake your head if I’m right,” Monique instructed.

Riley nodded, agreeing to answer Monique.

“Is it the Riding the Bull game?” Monique slowly asked in a soft tone.

Riley nodded. Monique immediately held her sister tightly as they began to cry.

“I’m sorry! I’m so sorry!” cried Riley, feeling guilty and ashamed.

“Riley, this is not your fault!” Monique said sternly. “Was it Josh?”

“He told me not to tell, or someone would die. I don’t want anyone to die!” Riley bawled.

"It's okay," cried Monique. "This is not your fault. Do you hear me, Riley?"

Riley nodded, still feeling guilty but relieved she told her sister.

"I have a secret," Monique said. "Josh played that game with me when I was 13 years old. Mom and Dad had a movie night, and Josh and I were alone downstairs. He made me pinky promise, but tonight, we are telling on him," Monique firmly stated.

"Wait! Someone will die if we tell! We will break the chain," Riley cried in fear.

"Riley, there was never a chain. Josh lied. He wanted to scare you so that you wouldn't tell on him."

Riley began crying even harder, disappointed she fell for his awful trick.

"Mom! Dad!" Monique shouted.

A few moments later, their parents came running into Riley's room.

"What's wrong?" Mrs. Cole asked, extremely concerned.

"What's going on?" Mr. Cole said.

"Can we all go to the living room? We need to talk to you," Monique said.

"Can't this wait until the morning?" Mr. Cole yawned. "Peanut, why are you crying?"

"Mom, Dad, Josh raped Riley," Monique blurted, coming right out with the truth, no longer holding on to fear or shame.

"What?" Mr. and Mrs. Cole shouted in unison.

"When? How? Where?" they demanded in a fury.

Mrs. Cole was in tears, trying to piece together the words to say to her daughter.

"Let's calm down," Mr. Cole instructed, trying to regain composure. "Peanut, talk to us. You know you can tell us anything. What happened, Honey?" Mr. Cole gently asked.

As Riley cried, she began telling her parents the events which occurred the previous day. Mrs. Cole rushed to Riley's side, with tears running down her face, and began holding her daughter.

"Monique, how did you know about this?" Mr. Cole asked.

"Daddy, Josh did it to me, too," cried Monique. "Ever since that day, many years ago, Josh acted as if nothing happened."

"Call the police right now," Mrs. Cole demanded to her husband, refusing to let this go on another minute. While the four of them waited for the police, they held each other tightly, crying and comforting one another.

When the police arrived, Riley gave her statement to the officer. Mrs. Cole instructed Riley to give the police her clothing from that day.

"Why do they need my clothes?" Riley asked in confusion.

"Good question, Sweetie. I'm sorry for not explaining, but your clothes will help the police find evidence or substances from his body. We also need you to get a physical at the hospital. When someone abuses another person, and they bravely tell the police, the police want to make sure your health is in good standing, so the doctors at the hospital will need to run a few tests."

The police took a statement from Monique, too.

"What now?" Riley asked Mrs. Cole as the police wrapped up their paperwork.

"Hopefully, Josh will go to jail," Mrs. Cole said sternly, "and you never have to worry about him hurting you or Monique again."

"We are so sorry this happened. We love you guys so much," Mr. Cole said, "and we couldn't be prouder that you told us about Josh."

As Monique, Riley, and Mr. and Mrs. Cole sat in the living room, Mr. Cole broke the silence, cleared his throat, and began to speak. “Girls, you did the right thing by telling us what happened. I can’t imagine your fear. Please know we are very proud of you. I want to let you know that it is always okay to say no, even to an adult. You are in charge of your body. If someone touches you or treats you inappropriately, or their actions or words make you uncomfortable, you are allowed to say no. Also, if someone asks you to touch them or another person, be sure to say no, as that is also not okay. There is nothing you could say to us that will make us love you less. Never let anyone convince you to keep a secret from us.”

Riley nodded as her father continued to talk about inappropriate touching and the importance of not keeping secrets. Surprisingly, Riley felt a bit better. She also felt a slight twinge of pride, knowing she bravely told her sister the truth and spoke up against Josh.

"My body is my body," Riley said, interrupting her dad, "and I know I can talk to you, Mom, and Monique about anything!"

Mrs. Cole smiled with tears in her eyes, and Mr. Cole cheered, "That's right, Baby! You can tell us anything."

"I'm proud of you," Monique whispered to her sister. "And I'm proud of you, too," Riley whispered back with a smile.

Lessons for a Lifetime

Fun secrets between friends, with no bodily or emotional harm, are good. However, if someone touches you inappropriately, do not keep this a secret, no matter what they say. Someone touching you without your permission is not okay or acceptable, no matter who it is. Talk to someone you trust. No means no! Also, remember to respect others' space and privacy too. Respect their request.

National Sexual Assault Hotline:
1-800-656-4673
www.rainn.org
www.stopitnow.org

Made in the USA
Middletown, DE
08 August 2024

58414886R00029